Disney
FROZEN II
MAD LIBS JUNIOR.

by Molly Reisner

MAD LIBS
An Imprint of Penguin Random House LLC, New York

Mad Libs format copyright © 2019 by Penguin Random House LLC. All rights reserved.

Concept created by Roger Price & Leonard Stern

Published by Mad Libs,
an imprint of Penguin Random House LLC, New York.
Printed in the USA.

Visit us online at www.penguinrandomhouse.com.

ISBN 9780593093917
1 3 5 7 9 10 8 6 4 2

MAD LIBS 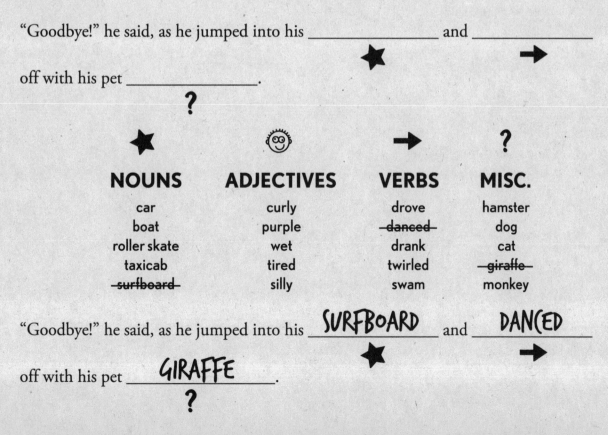 JUNIOR.

INSTRUCTIONS

MAD LIBS JUNIOR® is a game for kids who don't like games!
It can be played by one, two, three, four, or forty.

RIDICULOUSLY SIMPLE DIRECTIONS:

At the top of each page in this book, you will find four columns of words, each headed by
a symbol. Each symbol represents a part of speech. The symbols are:

NOUNS   **ADJECTIVES**   **VERBS**   **MISC.**

MAD LIBS JUNIOR® is fun to play with friends, but you can also play it by yourself!
To begin, look at the story on the page below. When you come to a blank space in the
story, look at the symbol that appears underneath. Then find the same symbol on this page
and pick a word that appears below the symbol. Put that word in the blank space, and
cross out the word, so you don't use it again. Continue doing this throughout the story
until you've filled in all the spaces. Finally, read your story aloud and laugh!

EXAMPLE:

"Goodbye!" he said, as he jumped into his _____ and _____

★   ➡

off with his pet _____.

?

★	😀	➡	?
NOUNS	**ADJECTIVES**	**VERBS**	**MISC.**
car	curly	drove	hamster
boat	purple	~~danced~~	dog
roller skate	wet	drank	cat
taxicab	tired	twirled	~~giraffe~~
~~surfboard~~	silly	swam	monkey

"Goodbye!" he said, as he jumped into his _SURFBOARD_ and _DANCED_

★   ➡

off with his pet _GIRAFFE_.

?

MAD LIBS ☺ JUNIOR.
QUICK REVIEW

In case you haven't learned about the parts of speech yet, here is a quick lesson:

A **NOUN** ★ is the name of a person, place, or thing. *Sidewalk, umbrella, bathtub,* and *roller skates* are nouns.

An **ADJECTIVE** ☺ describes a person, place, or thing. *Lumpy, soft, ugly, messy,* and *short* are adjectives.

A **VERB** → is an action word. *Run, jump,* and *swim* are verbs.

MISC. **?** can be any word at all. Some examples of a word that could be miscellaneous are: *nose, monkey, five,* and *blue.*

MAD LIBS JUNIOR® is fun to play with friends, but you can also play it by yourself! To begin, look at the story on the page below. When you come to a blank space in the story, look at the symbol that appears underneath. Then find the same symbol on this page and pick a word that appears below the symbol. Put that word in the blank space, and cross out the word, so you don't use it again. Continue doing this throughout the story until you've filled in all the spaces. Finally, read your story aloud and laugh!

SISTERS IN THE SNOW

★ NOUNS	☺ ADJECTIVES	→ VERBS	? MISC.
sock	dazzling	jumping	toes
yo-yo	creaky	gliding	feet
pencil	blue	weaving	elbows
ball	silly	napping	hair
muffin	bubbly	skating	noses
lantern	cloudy	shining	thumbs
birdhouse	amazing	throwing	knees
glitter	spicy	smashing	ankles
pineapple	soft	spinning	hands
microscope	magical	waiting	ears
sun	giant	itching	eyelashes
lollipop	magenta	skipping	arms

SISTERS IN THE SNOW

Early one morning, before their parents woke up, Elsa and her

little _____ ★ Anna held hands while _____ →

down the palace stairs to a/an _____ ☺ ballroom. "Do

the magic!" Anna squealed. Elsa spun her _____ ?

in circles, and snowflakes appeared! As her magic grew, the

snowflakes turned into a glowing snow-_____ ★ !

After _____ → high in the air, the snowball burst into a

_____ ★ shower. "This is _____ ☺ ," said Anna,

_____ → around the room. Elsa was ready to show Anna

more. With a stomp of her _____ ? , Elsa's _____ ☺

magic turned the floor into an ice-_____ → rink! The

sisters skated together, having the most _____ ☺ time in

their very own _____ ★ wonderland!

MAD LIBS JUNIOR® is fun to play with friends, but you can also play it by yourself! To begin, look at the story on the page below. When you come to a blank space in the story, look at the symbol that appears underneath. Then find the same symbol on this page and pick a word that appears below the symbol. Put that word in the blank space, and cross out the word, so you don't use it again. Continue doing this throughout the story until you've filled in all the spaces. Finally, read your story aloud and laugh!

WINTER THINGS TO DO IN SNOWY ARENDELLE

★ NOUNS	☺ ADJECTIVES	→ VERBS	? MISC.
computers	scratchy	hopping	1 million
shoes	shimmering	swimming	5
jelly beans	teensy	stretching	14,028
scarves	cold	sprinting	76
ice cubes	purple	flying	239
soccer balls	quiet	skating	18
tents	cozy	singing	3
gloves	empty	hiking	902
hairbrushes	toasty	sneezing	5,000
plums	muddy	cooking	7 billion
diamonds	bouncy	blinking	28
boats	sticky	smiling	800

MAD LIBS JUNIOR.

WINTER THINGS TO DO IN SNOWY ARENDELLE

_____ into chilly Arendelle anytime soon?
➡

Check out our top _____ things to do when it's
?

freezing _____ out! *Brrrrr!* Don't forget to pack a few
☺

_____ to keep you nice and _____ .
★   ☺

1. You won't want to miss _____ on the frozen lake!
➡

Bundle up with a/an _____ hat and a cozy pair of
☺

_____ because it's colder than a snowman's nose!
★

2. Take a break from _____ snowmen and making
➡

snow _____ with a cup of _____ chocolate!
★   ☺

3. Need some _____ for a _____ trip? Wandering
★   ➡

Oaken's Trading Post and Sauna has _____ really
?

_____ ones for sale. Plus the sauna will warm you
☺

right up!

MAD LIBS JUNIOR® is fun to play with friends, but you can also play it by yourself! To begin, look at the story on the page below. When you come to a blank space in the story, look at the symbol that appears underneath. Then find the same symbol on this page and pick a word that appears below the symbol. Put that word in the blank space, and cross out the word, so you don't use it again. Continue doing this throughout the story until you've filled in all the spaces. Finally, read your story aloud and laugh!

HOW TO HARVEST ICE

★ NOUNS	☺ ADJECTIVES	➡ VERBS	? MISC.
cupcakes	fluffy	mash	slowest
roses	hard	slice	coziest
spikes	cushy	skip	itchiest
pot holders	rippled	crawl	strongest
hands	weird	chomp	craziest
apricots	striped	dart	best
dolls	funny	lift	newest
tights	broken	howl	driest
leaves	rocky	tap-dance	safest
blocks	frozen	bake	oldest
crowns	sharp	look	finest
night-lights	crunchy	poke	widest

MAD LIBS JUNIOR

HOW TO HARVEST ICE

Learn how to _____ ➡ through the cold,

_____ 😎 ice just like a pro ice harvester!

Step 1: Bundle up in your _____ ❓ clothes so your

_____ ⭐ don't freeze!

Step 2: Make sure you have _____ 😎 tools for the job.

You'll need some long, _____ 😎 -toothed _____ ⭐

to cut the ice, shoes with _____ ⭐ on the bottom so you

don't slip, and a very _____ 😎 reindeer to pull the sled.

Step 3: Using your _____ ❓ hand, push the saw deep

into the water's _____ 😎 surface. Then _____ ➡

back and forth until a chunk of ice separates.

Step 4: Carefully _____ ➡ the ice out of the water and

onto your sled. You did it!

MAD LIBS JUNIOR® is fun to play with friends, but you can also play it by yourself! To begin, look at the story on the page below. When you come to a blank space in the story, look at the symbol that appears underneath. Then find the same symbol on this page and pick a word that appears below the symbol. Put that word in the blank space, and cross out the word, so you don't use it again. Continue doing this throughout the story until you've filled in all the spaces. Finally, read your story aloud and laugh!

CARROT STEW RECIPE

★ NOUNS	😀 ADJECTIVES	➡ VERBS	? MISC.
walnuts	yellow	shrinking	Z
helicopters	sour	wiping	D
potatoes	glossy	sneezing	Q
worms	puffy	stirring	P
toothbrushes	dry	stewing	A
telephones	oily	poking	Y
coconuts	sunny	yawning	G
underwear	wooden	bouncing	B
roller coasters	hairy	sobbing	J
oranges	burnt	skipping	W
pebbles	fresh	giggling	M
rain boots	crunchy	twisting	C

MAD LIBS JUNIOR

CARROT STEW RECIPE

What is Sven the reindeer's favorite snack? _____

carrots, of course! Cook up your own orange _____

with this vitamin _____—packed stew that will

have you (and Sven) _____ the bowl clean! Chop up

one _____ onion, two large _____, and

five peeled _____. Heat oil in a pot and then add the

_____. Keep _____ with a spoon until

they get soft. Toss in the _____ and cover with water.

Cook until everything is _____ and then mix in three

table-_____ of flour. Throw in tomatoes and leave it

_____ for five more minutes. Serve immediately

and your guests will give it a/an _____+!

MAD LIBS JUNIOR® is fun to play with friends, but you can also play it by yourself! To begin, look at the story on the page below. When you come to a blank space in the story, look at the symbol that appears underneath. Then find the same symbol on this page and pick a word that appears below the symbol. Put that word in the blank space, and cross out the word, so you don't use it again. Continue doing this throughout the story until you've filled in all the spaces. Finally, read your story aloud and laugh!

PARTY TIME, BY ANNA

★ NOUNS	☺ ADJECTIVES	→ VERBS	? MISC.
ice pop	frizzy	whirling	14
spatula	squishy	snapping	900
pillow	prickly	crawling	2
blimp	purple	dancing	87
garage	gassy	playing	3 million
gate	lively	cooking	4,001
ponytail	rotten	skiing	567
package	funny	laughing	0
feather	teensy	scooping	1 trillion
hot tub	boring	crunching	999
T-shirt	crazy	falling	11
prince	deep	juggling	200,008

MAD LIBS JUNIOR.
PARTY TIME, BY ANNA

Castle life can be a bit quiet and _____ 😊 , but not

today! In just _____ ❓ hours, the castle's _____ ⭐

will open for Elsa's coronation! My _____ ⭐ , Elsa, is going

to become queen today. Which means real, _____ 😊

people are coming to celebrate! _____ 😊 , right? When's

the last time that happened? _____ ❓ years ago?! For

the first time in forever, there'll be _____ ➡ in the

ballroom. I'll see people smiling, and _____ ➡ , and

(*yum!*) I can already smell the _____ 😊 cake baking in

the _____ ⭐ ! I can't stop _____ ➡ who I'll meet

tonight! Maybe it's someone _____ 😊 . Either way,

I'm going to have a _____ 😊 time _____ ➡

with everyone!

MAD LIBS JUNIOR® is fun to play with friends, but you can also play it by yourself! To begin, look at the story on the page below. When you come to a blank space in the story, look at the symbol that appears underneath. Then find the same symbol on this page and pick a word that appears below the symbol. Put that word in the blank space, and cross out the word, so you don't use it again. Continue doing this throughout the story until you've filled in all the spaces. Finally, read your story aloud and laugh!

THE WEASEL OF WESELTON

★ NOUNS	☻ ADJECTIVES	→ VERBS	? MISC.
llamas	hairy	breathing	thumb
sweaters	fantastic	waltzing	eyelash
frozen peas	sloppy	frowning	elbow
daffodils	confident	diving	nostril
bodyguards	friendly	flipping	ankle
erasers	wacky	sprinting	heart
clowns	floppy	ice-skating	face
cheeseburgers	happy	rowing	hand
drums	fizzy	spinning	earlobe
treasures	scratchy	dreaming	neck
garbage	quick	trading	chin
gumdrops	sleepy	cleaning	pinkie toe

MAD LIBS JUNIOR.
THE WEASEL OF WESELTON

Who is sneaky, overly _____ 😀 , and wants all of

Arendelle's _____ ★ ? The Duke of Weselton, of course!

It's safe to say the Duke's _____ ? is full of greed. And,

between you and me, he's also a really _____ 😀 dancer!

At Elsa's coronation, while _____ → with Anna, he

twirled around on his _____ ? while _____ →

with his _____ ? . It was . . . _____ 😀 . After

Elsa shot frozen _____ ★ out of her _____ ? ,

the Duke was rude and called her "a _____ 😀 monster."

He even ordered his _____ ★ to go after her! Luckily,

the Duke's plan blew up in his _____ ? . Queen Elsa

stood tall and banned Weselton from trading _____ ★

with Arendelle ever again! Bye-bye, Duke!

MAD LIBS JUNIOR® is fun to play with friends, but you can also play it by yourself! To begin, look at the story on the page below. When you come to a blank space in the story, look at the symbol that appears underneath. Then find the same symbol on this page and pick a word that appears below the symbol. Put that word in the blank space, and cross out the word, so you don't use it again. Continue doing this throughout the story until you've filled in all the spaces. Finally, read your story aloud and laugh!

CHILL IN THE AIR

★ NOUNS	☺ ADJECTIVES	→ VERBS	? MISC.
pickle	tasty	spun	slowly
french toast	gooey	snapped	thoughtfully
hero	gross	wished	suddenly
armadillo	slimy	trotted	happily
camera	lumpy	cartwheeled	loudly
pen	goofy	flipped	quickly
kitten	strange	thumped	meanly
kingdom	charming	cried	totally
caterpillar	warm	sprinted	sadly
juice box	groovy	whirled	excitedly
backpack	chunky	sailed	nicely
swimsuit	clunky	blinked	weirdly

Once upon a/an _____ , Princess Anna met a

_____ prince named Hans. He was _____ ,

funny, and sweet—she _____ fell in love. After Elsa

froze Arendelle and _____ _____ away,

Anna knew she needed to follow her. Without anyone to take

care of Arendelle, Anna put Hans in charge. She trusted he

would keep Arendelle safe and _____ . But, when

Anna needed an act of _____ love to save her freezing

_____ , Hans _____ . He only wanted to

be the _____ of Arendelle and needed Anna out of

his way! It wasn't true _____ at all! What Hans didn't

know was that Elsa could save Anna's _____ , because

_____ love between sisters is the strongest bond of all!

MAD LIBS JUNIOR® is fun to play with friends, but you can also play it by yourself! To begin, look at the story on the page below. When you come to a blank space in the story, look at the symbol that appears underneath. Then find the same symbol on this page and pick a word that appears below the symbol. Put that word in the blank space, and cross out the word, so you don't use it again. Continue doing this throughout the story until you've filled in all the spaces. Finally, read your story aloud and laugh!

UP THE NORTH MOUNTAIN WE GO!

★ NOUNS	☺ ADJECTIVES	➡ VERBS	? MISC.
handkerchief	fuzzy	sniffing	Hello
glue stick	fluffy	wandering	Greetings
sponge	glittery	skipping	Oh yeah
castle	glorious	crawling	No thanks
sneaker	bubbly	barking	See ya
milkshake	glowing	hiking	Oh my
bagel	boring	humming	Yikes
moose	teensy	yawning	Goodbye
princess	warm	shivering	Hooray
pool	sticky	floating	Boo-hoo
tadpole	crazy	swirling	Bye-bye
lollipop	smooth	biking	Wow

MAD LIBS JUNIOR.

UP THE NORTH MOUNTAIN WE GO!

I was _____ ➡ around in the snow when I saw a girl, a

_____ ★ , and a big _____ ☺ -looking donkey

(who turned out to be a _____ ★ named Kristoff).

When they saw me, they screamed, "_____ ?!" They had

never seen a _____ ➡ snowman before, but we became

_____ ☺ friends after Anna gave me a _____ ★

for a nose! My new friends were _____ ➡ for Anna's

sister, Elsa. They needed her to change the _____ ★ into

summer, and asked for my help to find her. Me? Help bring

back the most _____ ☺ season of all? _____ ? !

I led my friends all the way up the North _____ ★ ,

_____ ➡ about all of the _____ ☺ things to do

in summer.

MAD LIBS JUNIOR® is fun to play with friends, but you can also play it by yourself! To begin, look at the story on the page below. When you come to a blank space in the story, look at the symbol that appears underneath. Then find the same symbol on this page and pick a word that appears below the symbol. Put that word in the blank space, and cross out the word, so you don't use it again. Continue doing this throughout the story until you've filled in all the spaces. Finally, read your story aloud and laugh!

KRISTOFF'S ROCKIN' FAMILY

★ NOUNS	☺ ADJECTIVES	→ VERBS	? MISC.
owl	powerful	learning	700
rock	caring	living	45
tutu	crusty	healing	1
crystal	strong	leaping	1,999
friend	square	dancing	3,001
sock	merry	standing	17
gummy bear	fancy	snacking	579
mountain	salty	snapping	1 billion
cloud	young	scrunching	86
tennis ball	sweet	laughing	20,000
diary	prickly	smudging	340,034
kid	round	napping	7

MAD LIBS JUNIOR.
KRISTOFF'S ROCKIN' FAMILY

Meet the trolls—a group of friendly, _____

creatures who live in the Valley of the _____ Rock.

Grand Pabbie: A wise, _____ troll. He uses his

magical and _____ powers for helping others and

_____ into the future.

Bulda: Warm and _____ , she is like a/an

_____ to Kristoff. Bulda adopted him when he was only

a/an _____ -year-old _____ !

Cliff: Married to his _____ -heart Bulda for over

_____ years, Cliff loves her more than anything. He's a

rock-solid kind of _____ !

Little Rock: He may still be _____ , but this young

troll is proud to have earned his Level 1 Crystals!

MAD LIBS JUNIOR® is fun to play with friends, but you can also play it by yourself! To begin, look at the story on the page below. When you come to a blank space in the story, look at the symbol that appears underneath. Then find the same symbol on this page and pick a word that appears below the symbol. Put that word in the blank space, and cross out the word, so you don't use it again. Continue doing this throughout the story until you've filled in all the spaces. Finally, read your story aloud and laugh!

FOREVER FAMILY

★ NOUNS	☺ ADJECTIVES	→ VERBS	? MISC.
cookies	funny	jumped	oldest
books	crumbly	drummed	strongest
turnips	soapy	stretched	creakiest
stripes	loyal	chatted	best
bears	annoyed	hid	shiniest
carousels	distant	waddled	friendliest
pinwheels	early	flew	quietest
curtains	close	drove	fluffiest
burritos	sad	skipped	sharpest
rubies	crowded	hiccuped	silliest
daffodils	messy	honked	scariest
zippers	eternal	galloped	driest

MAD LIBS 😊 JUNIOR.
FOREVER FAMILY

When Anna and Elsa were young _____, they were

as _____ as sisters could be! But things changed

when Elsa _____ in her room . . . for years. Anna felt

confused and _____ but never gave up hope that they

would be close _____ again. After Elsa showed her

magic and _____ away from Arendelle, Anna braved

dangerous, _____ weather to find her. When she

did, Elsa pushed Anna away with the _____ ice bolt

ever—it froze her heart! Even in her _____, weakest

moment, Anna wanted only to protect her sister, especially from

Hans's evil plan. Anna's _____ love for Elsa is what

saved their relationship and brought sunny _____

back to Arendelle!

MAD LIBS JUNIOR® is fun to play with friends, but you can also play it by yourself! To begin, look at the story on the page below. When you come to a blank space in the story, look at the symbol that appears underneath. Then find the same symbol on this page and pick a word that appears below the symbol. Put that word in the blank space, and cross out the word, so you don't use it again. Continue doing this throughout the story until you've filled in all the spaces. Finally, read your story aloud and laugh!

AMAZING ANNA

★ NOUNS	☺ ADJECTIVES	➔ VERBS	? MISC.
phone	purple	scratch	shoulder
buddy	jolly	laugh	nose
toaster	lucky	meow	knuckle
giraffe	crunchy	feel	cheek
goofball	splendid	sniff	chin
cabbage	hilarious	mix	tummy
trumpet	special	wink	knee
trampoline	right	try	eyebrow
goblin	grumpy	fold	head
woodpecker	rosy	sob	hair
hammer	clumsy	scrunch	thumb
ski pole	fierce	leap	heart

MAD LIBS JUNIOR.
AMAZING ANNA

When Kristoff is in need of some advice, he turns to his trusty

_____ , Sven. Listen in as he talks about all the ways ⭐

Anna holds a _____ place in his _____ ! ☺ ❓

So, Sven, I'm wondering what you think of Anna. Yeah, I thought

she was _____ too at first. Kind of _____ ? ☺ ☺

But also wonderfully . . . _____ . Brave. Amazing. ☺

I've never met a _____ who can _____ ⭐ ➡

like she does! No, my _____ isn't blushing, Sven! Do ❓

you think she likes me back? What about that _____ , ⭐

Hans, she wants to marry? You're right. I should tell her how I

_____ . When the time is _____ , I will. ➡ ☺

Thanks for the advice, Sven. You always come through!

MAD LIBS JUNIOR® is fun to play with friends, but you can also play it by yourself! To begin, look at the story on the page below. When you come to a blank space in the story, look at the symbol that appears underneath. Then find the same symbol on this page and pick a word that appears below the symbol. Put that word in the blank space, and cross out the word, so you don't use it again. Continue doing this throughout the story until you've filled in all the spaces. Finally, read your story aloud and laugh!

SPIRITS IN THE FOREST

★ NOUNS	☺ ADJECTIVES	→ VERBS	? MISC.
pajamas	boring	grilling	950
elephants	silly	pouncing	14
hills	magical	writing	11
swimsuits	short	arguing	5,003
bananas	terrible	hugging	88
french fries	silver	clapping	777,777
leggings	confused	snoozing	2,468
daughters	dreary	pouring	9,753
grandmas	blurry	braiding	3
keys	slimy	twisting	624
tulips	nice	baking	500,005
bridges	spicy	fidgeting	10

MAD LIBS JUNIOR.
SPIRITS IN THE FOREST

When Anna and Elsa were young, their father told them a story

about the _____ Forest outside Arendelle's gates . . .

A long, _____ time ago, there were _____ from

the north called the Northuldra. They lived peacefully in the forest

with the _____ spirits of nature: Wind, Fire, Earth, and

_____ . King Runeard invited the Northuldra to see the

dam he had built for them as a symbol of peace. It should have been

a _____ celebration. Instead, the Northuldra began

fighting us. The spirits, angered with all the _____ ,

surrounded the forest with a _____ mist—trapping the

Northuldra and some of our own _____ inside. We'd love

to reunite with our lost Arendellians, but there's _____

magic that stops anyone from going in.

MAD LIBS JUNIOR® is fun to play with friends, but you can also play it by yourself! To begin, look at the story on the page below. When you come to a blank space in the story, look at the symbol that appears underneath. Then find the same symbol on this page and pick a word that appears below the symbol. Put that word in the blank space, and cross out the word, so you don't use it again. Continue doing this throughout the story until you've filled in all the spaces. Finally, read your story aloud and laugh!

THE LEGEND OF THE RIVER

★ NOUNS	😀 ADJECTIVES	→ VERBS	? MISC.
raspberry	delightful	jump	Jenny
bathtub	freezing	disappear	Olga
mountain	mythical	grow	Penelope
poodle	real	nibble	Ava
blanket	stinky	slide	Iduna
log	sparkling	itch	Nancy
river	chewing	change	Willa
broom	sweet	break	Chloe
pony	tiny	smile	Agnarr
lasagna	magenta	fade	Connie
cake	dusty	stitch	Emily
microphone	crabby	blink	Izzie

MAD LIBS JUNIOR.
THE LEGEND OF THE RIVER

One night at bedtime, Queen _____ **?** shared the

legend of a _____ 😊 river with her girls, Anna and

_____ **?** . Here is what she said . . . *Way up north,*

beyond the lakes and the forests that surround Arendelle, there is

thought to be a _____ 😎 , magical river called Ahtohallan.

*No one knows for certain if _____ **?** is _____ 😊*

or not. This _____ ⭐ is full of mystery—it knows

everything and can _____ ➡️ the answer to any problem.

If the _____ ⭐ calls you, you must _____ ➡️ .

But beware. It is easy to _____ ➡️ if you spend too much

time getting lost in the _____ 😎 old memories the

_____ ⭐ can show you.

MAD LIBS JUNIOR® is fun to play with friends, but you can also play it by yourself! To begin, look at the story on the page below. When you come to a blank space in the story, look at the symbol that appears underneath. Then find the same symbol on this page and pick a word that appears below the symbol. Put that word in the blank space, and cross out the word, so you don't use it again. Continue doing this throughout the story until you've filled in all the spaces. Finally, read your story aloud and laugh!

MAKING MAGIC

★ NOUNS	☺ ADJECTIVES	→ VERBS	? MISC.
bubbles	upside-down	wave	bam
tacos	mellow	clap	whoosh
socks	dirty	smash	vroom
clothes	soggy	bend	hooray
daisies	favorite	twirl	freeze
grasshoppers	healthy	flip	hello
jelly beans	faraway	drop	whoa
igloos	colorful	float	yay
eyes	wrinkly	curl	mmm
crayons	knotty	squeeze	achoo
pictures	dazzling	snap	bravo
sofas	sweaty	grab	woo-hoo

Elsa has the _____ ability to turn _____ into snow and _____! If you had a magical talent, what would it be? How would it _____? Here are some _____ examples to get you started!

1. _____ your hands three times and _____!—your _____ are put away in your dresser and your room is all _____!

2. Chant _____ twice, _____ a wand in the air, and now you can eat all the _____ for dessert you want! Yum.

3. Need a ride somewhere? Just whisper your _____ destination into the mirror, close your _____, and when you open them, you'll be there!

MAD LIBS JUNIOR® is fun to play with friends, but you can also play it by yourself! To begin, look at the story on the page below. When you come to a blank space in the story, look at the symbol that appears underneath. Then find the same symbol on this page and pick a word that appears below the symbol. Put that word in the blank space, and cross out the word, so you don't use it again. Continue doing this throughout the story until you've filled in all the spaces. Finally, read your story aloud and laugh!

OLAF'S GOT QUESTIONS!

★ NOUNS	☺ ADJECTIVES	➡ VERBS	? MISC.
waters	crumbly	flip	10
carrots	cold	dance	24
toasters	wet	run	99
computers	small	melt	16
friends	goofy	yell	11
eggs	sleepy	study	252
dreams	happy	snore	900
pinecones	lumpy	nap	62
snowflakes	smart	swim	45
elephants	playful	talk	101
raisins	lopsided	shop	3
teeth	different	play	658

MAD LIBS ⦿ JUNIOR.
OLAF'S GOT QUESTIONS!

Olaf joined his _____ Anna, Elsa, Kristoff, and Sven

on a very long and _____ journey to the Enchanted

Forest. He helped pass the time by sharing _____

_____ trivia _____. Here are his favorites:

1. Did you know that _____ can remember stuff?

2. Did you know that gorillas _____ when they feel

_____?

3. Did you know we _____ _____ million

times a day?

4. Did you know that donkeys _____ but

_____ don't?

5. Did you know a wombat's _____ look like squares?

MAD LIBS JUNIOR® is fun to play with friends, but you can also play it by yourself! To begin, look at the story on the page below. When you come to a blank space in the story, look at the symbol that appears underneath. Then find the same symbol on this page and pick a word that appears below the symbol. Put that word in the blank space, and cross out the word, so you don't use it again. Continue doing this throughout the story until you've filled in all the spaces. Finally, read your story aloud and laugh!

ELSA'S SPECIAL SOUND

★ NOUNS	☺ ADJECTIVES	→ VERBS	? MISC.
pillow	smelly	pounding	earlobe
cupcake	thirsty	napping	eyebrow
flamingo	clear	frolicking	neck
baseball cap	soft	spreading	heart
songbird	catchy	running	belly button
banjo	nutty	skipping	pinkie toe
wind chime	happy	shaking	shoulder
queen	spooky	picnicking	leg
vase	weird	spinning	knee
highlighter	cool	wobbling	hand
kitten	special	splashing	elbow
smoke alarm	greasy	twitching	lip

Things have been pretty _____ here in Arendelle! I'm

not sure if my _____ **?** is playing tricks on me, but I've

been hearing this _____ sound lately. It's a mysterious

yet _____ sound . . . like a _____ ★ singing

from a distant place. And when I hear it, my _____ **?**

starts _____ ➡ and I feel like _____ ➡ away to

find out where it's coming from! Why is it _____ ➡ me?

Can anyone else hear its _____ call? My kingdom

needs a _____ ★ , but my _____ **?** tells me

I must answer the _____ call. If I do, maybe I'll

discover why I have _____ abilities. Maybe there's an

answer _____ ➡ for me.

MAD LIBS JUNIOR® is fun to play with friends, but you can also play it by yourself! To begin, look at the story on the page below. When you come to a blank space in the story, look at the symbol that appears underneath. Then find the same symbol on this page and pick a word that appears below the symbol. Put that word in the blank space, and cross out the word, so you don't use it again. Continue doing this throughout the story until you've filled in all the spaces. Finally, read your story aloud and laugh!

WHICH SPIRIT ARE YOU?

★ NOUNS	😊 ADJECTIVES	➡ VERBS	? MISC.
flute	polite	blow	no way
soap	light	shake	never
magic wand	fizzy	squish	nah
rose	zippy	run	nope
pumpkin	bubbly	dance	seriously?
grass	spiky	relax	that's a no
whale	jealous	bend	negative
candy cane	brave	bathe	n to the o
daisy	fun	march	nuh-uh
telephone	wacky	float	no thanks
cabbage	excellent	shimmy	pass
lunch box	frilly	scuttle	no chance

MAD LIBS JUNIOR.
WHICH SPIRIT ARE YOU?

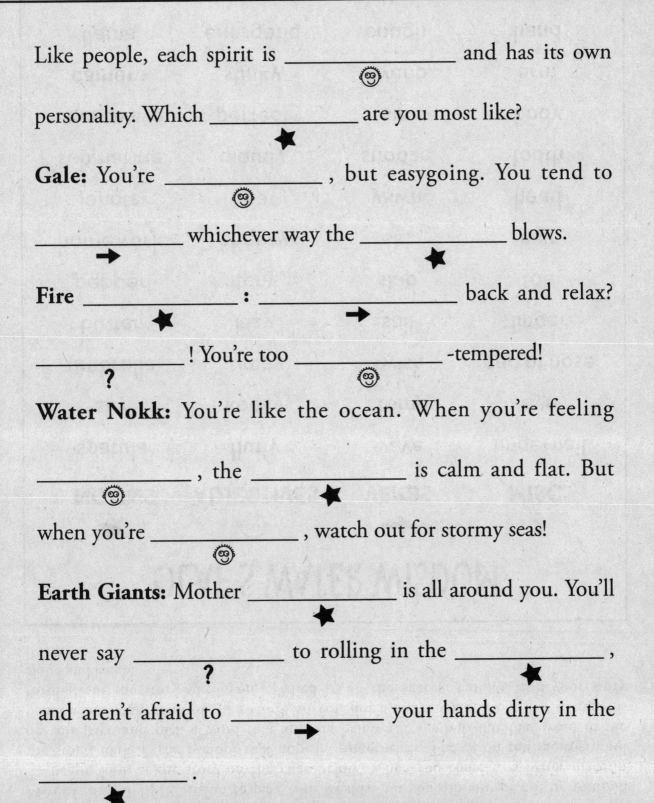

Like people, each spirit is _____ and has its own

personality. Which _____ are you most like?

Gale: You're _____ , but easygoing. You tend to

_____ whichever way the _____ blows.

Fire _____ : _____ back and relax?

_____ ! You're too _____ -tempered!

Water Nokk: You're like the ocean. When you're feeling

_____ , the _____ is calm and flat. But

when you're _____ , watch out for stormy seas!

Earth Giants: Mother _____ is all around you. You'll

never say _____ to rolling in the _____ ,

and aren't afraid to _____ your hands dirty in the

_____ .

MAD LIBS JUNIOR® is fun to play with friends, but you can also play it by yourself! To begin, look at the story on the page below. When you come to a blank space in the story, look at the symbol that appears underneath. Then find the same symbol on this page and pick a word that appears below the symbol. Put that word in the blank space, and cross out the word, so you don't use it again. Continue doing this throughout the story until you've filled in all the spaces. Finally, read your story aloud and laugh!

OLAF'S WATER WISDOM

★ NOUNS	☺ ADJECTIVES	→ VERBS	? MISC.
spatula	fluffy	wave	fingernail
sky	kooky	stomp	eye
umbrella	jumpy	swish	carrot nose
butter	lazy	sail	finger
pepper	itchy	skip	toe
homework	cheery	ski	hair
jungle	neat	yawn	head
submarine	cloudy	snooze	tooth
microwave	perfect	sip	body
camera	stinky	sweep	arm
llama	energetic	cough	hand
cheese	angry	chew	tummy

MAD LIBS JUNIOR.
OLAF'S WATER WISDOM

Water is _____ ! It's so smart and _____ —

it even remembers stuff! Oh, I just remembered the last time I

went _____ -skating with Anna. I tried to do a triple

_____ and fell on my _____ ! I was

feeling embarrassed, but luckily no one saw me _____ .

Wait a second! If ice is frozen water, it must have remembered

my _____ ! It's a good thing the ice was a/an

_____ friend and decided not to tell anyone. Wow,

water really is _____ ! Hey! If my _____

is made of snow, which is also frozen water, then I'm made

up of water! That probably explains why I have such a/an

_____ memory.

From FROZEN 2 MAD LIBS JUNIOR® • Copyright © 2019 Disney Enterprises, Inc.
All rights reserved. Published by Mad Libs, an imprint of Penguin Random House LLC.

MAD LIBS JUNIOR® is fun to play with friends, but you can also play it by yourself! To begin, look at the story on the page below. When you come to a blank space in the story, look at the symbol that appears underneath. Then find the same symbol on this page and pick a word that appears below the symbol. Put that word in the blank space, and cross out the word, so you don't use it again. Continue doing this throughout the story until you've filled in all the spaces. Finally, read your story aloud and laugh!

FEELING LOST IN THE LOST CAVERNS

★ NOUNS	☺ ADJECTIVES	➡ VERBS	? MISC.
wedding	bright	sniffed	backyard
wasp	giggly	biked	Mars
gorilla	cool	danced	sandbox
sister	peaceful	hopped	cave
gopher	chatty	kicked	classroom
pal	brave	spun	bathtub
sun	squeaky	rolled	carnival
mall	stuffy	stuck	bank
sandwich	quiet	looked	closet
clown	shimmery	yodeled	river
lantern	snowy	swam	North Pole
playground	jumpy	twitched	Arendelle

MAD LIBS JUNIOR.
FEELING LOST IN THE LOST CAVERNS

It was a long and _____ journey to help Elsa get to

(the) _____ . The scariest part was when Olaf
?

and I got _____ in the Lost Caverns. It was dark

and _____ down there! I _____ around

for a way out, but everything was so _____ . I was

even more worried about Elsa! I didn't know if she was safe

out in (the) _____ . What if I never saw my
?

_____ again? I felt so _____ and alone,
★

but luckily, I had my _____ Olaf by my side. We
★

_____ together because that's what friends do. And

just when I thought we would be _____ forever, my

_____ _____ pointed to the way out!
★

MAD LIBS JUNIOR® is fun to play with friends, but you can also play it by yourself! To begin, look at the story on the page below. When you come to a blank space in the story, look at the symbol that appears underneath. Then find the same symbol on this page and pick a word that appears below the symbol. Put that word in the blank space, and cross out the word, so you don't use it again. Continue doing this throughout the story until you've filled in all the spaces. Finally, read your story aloud and laugh!

DO YOU BELIEVE IN MAGIC?

★ NOUNS	☺ ADJECTIVES	→ VERBS	? MISC.
wizards	awesome	bounce	yeah
illusions	pointless	feel	yup
pizzas	hilarious	slurp	of course
dragons	crazy	smell	absolutely
pickles	real	freeze	oh yeah
jeans	sparkly	solve	yes please
cashews	soft	burp	for sure
doves	tired	melt	definitely
bunnies	hokey	snort	uh-huh
woodchucks	boring	spray	yeehaw
horses	electric	wash	yes sir
sandals	jiggly	shuffle	yah

MAD LIBS JUNIOR.
DO YOU BELIEVE IN MAGIC?

Are you a true magic believer like Honeymaren or do you

_____ ➡️ _____ it's just a bunch of tricks and _____ ⭐ _____ ,

like King Runeard? _____ ➡️ _____ these questions to find out!

1. When a magician makes a dozen _____ ⭐ _____

disappear, do you try to figure out how she does it?

(a) _____ ❓ _____ !

(b) Of course not, it's magic!

2. When you finally _____ ➡️ _____ **the** _____ ⭐ _____

you've been looking for, do you think it's magic at work?

(a) No, but it makes me feel _____ 😊 _____ !

(b) Well, _____ ❓ _____ !

If you answered *b* for both questions, then you get an A for

believing magic is _____ 😊 _____ !

MAD LIBS JUNIOR® is fun to play with friends, but you can also play it by yourself! To begin, look at the story on the page below. When you come to a blank space in the story, look at the symbol that appears underneath. Then find the same symbol on this page and pick a word that appears below the symbol. Put that word in the blank space, and cross out the word, so you don't use it again. Continue doing this throughout the story until you've filled in all the spaces. Finally, read your story aloud and laugh!

NORTHULDRA VS. ARENDELLIANS

★ NOUNS	😀 ADJECTIVES	→ VERBS	? MISC.
gumballs	brave	discovered	2
reindeer	funky	fried	22
blueberries	cheerful	fluffed	222
pretzels	bright	doodled	2,425
dogs	scared	danced	12
sisters	curly	napped	300,003
friends	true	skipped	99,999
family	square	nibbled	44
doctors	moody	hiccuped	63
tomatoes	fuzzy	flipped	50
tigers	busy	yodeled	8,040
sunglasses	tall	laughed	175

_____ years ago the _____ built the

?

Northuldra a dam as a sign of friendship. When the dam

was finished, the Arendellians _____ a party to

celebrate. _____ from all over the land were invited!

People _____ and had a _____ time, until

a fight broke out! The battle made the _____ of

the forest very _____—so they put a mist around

the _____ Forest to trap the people inside. King

Agnarr, who was only _____ years old, would have

?

been _____ in the mist, but a _____

Northuldra girl saved him. She _____ him even though

their people were fighting each other. She _____

bravery beyond her years by doing the right thing.

Download Mad Libs today!

Join the millions of Mad Libs fans creating wacky and wonderful stories on our apps!